A Fervour of Bee

Bhasrutha Reddy

BookLeaf Publishing

Presentation by *BookLeaf Publishing*

Web: www.bookleafpub.com

E-mail: info@bookleafpub.com

ISBN: 9789357217910

First edition 2023

DEDICATION

I thank my parents today for their blessings and the constant support that they have been for me who inspired me and encouraged me to fly towards my dreams. Thank you for trusting me.

I also want to Thank all my Family and Friends for showering endless love and hope upon me in every situation.

To the Beautiful Souls in my life,

Dear Mom,Dad and Brother

 I love you so much for being the reason behind my smile and happiness. You guys are the best.

'THIS IS MY FIRST EVER BOOK AS AN AUTHOR'

This book is dedicated to everyone who suffer in silence.

A fervour of Bee is a non fictional story book of poems about an insect called Bee. The intent behind a Bee is,what if Bee is a human who has emotions in it (him/her) and how would be the challenging life for it. Here we go with a pinch of inches of soul-stirring tiers.

The nature of this book is,every page can sound like a voice of Bee.Yes,its communicating with you. You wonder if I'm writing about you. Yes,I am.

And one day,she decided herself that she could tell someone the whole story of the why she is and the way she is.

There is a saying which I heard like'Not enough people talk about how mentally and physically exhausting anxiety can be.Your nervous system will really be in shambles. You're tired all of the time, your stomach in knots, and your heart racing.This is why daily, conscious self-care is so important' and that's absolutely true.

You worry about your trauma. Anxiety pushes you into the state of feeling like being upset,offended,annoyed and disappointed drowning with a burden of insecurities.

You yourself have to Heal You. Self motivation is the best confidence power in everyone's life.

You should give yourself the same kindness you give to others.

A little progress each day adds up to big results.

PREFACE

An Introspective Soul,
Overcoming the Stigma of mental Illness.
My mental Health is the Strength of my life.
In the process of Healing the little girl finally
found herself.
I will never give up.I will fight for myself.
Am the warrior.

The depth in my thoughts can relate you.

Few Excruciating stories end where people are characterized by deep, long lasting feelings of despair.
Every person is rendered by pure emotions in and out especially who is so loquacious.
A person who always refute to proselytize their twinge to either one or none being apathetic is a sign of depression. Feelings had spread and the emotions are misled.
What you perceive or what your premise is not true. There is always a loud voice for silence.
Don't be impertinent towards the heart sayings.

Every soul needs time, softness and patience.A lot of self motivation.

Remind yourself that you are not an empty shell,you are protecting a pearl.

DREAMGOALS

In the river of life,
The destiny and time tests you with the obstacles
in a way throughout your patience,your
strength,your courage and your tolerance.
It hits each and every root source.
The existence gives you the sleepless
nights,fearful thoughts,sweet memories,peace of
mind and many more feelings which gets faded
away within a period.
The essence of life is to stay firm and
enthusiastic to confront the consequences with
the spirit and fight with it.
The day when you make your life circumstances
a positive approach is the day where you will get
succeeded in your future. Your victory will
inspire many.
Set a strong goal for your success.
Make boundaries in advance.

WHEN SOMETHING IS
BETTER THAN
NOTHING
THEN MAKE
YOUR SOMETHING TO
BE EVERYTHING IF
YOUR DETERMINATION

IS THE
BEST THING.
NEVER GIVE UPON YOUR
FAILURES.ACCEPT IT UNTIL YOUR
IMPERFECTIONS MAKES
YOU THE PERFECT
DECISION.

You have to work for what you want,So far so
good.
All you need to do is Focus on the Goals with
Discipline,Dedication and Determination.
Don't Procrastinate your schedules. Time has no
limitations,once its gone it never comes back.
Set your goals wisely. Strive for progress not
perfection.
Persistence should work like a sense in our mind
in the journey of Success path.
Nothing is Impossible. Don't quit.
Make your Obstacles a favourite chapter in your
life,it gives a matured solution for everything.

DREAMGOALS

Let your wisdom begin with the Persistence.
Take every oppurtunity to prove what you are.

What is Firmness?
Firmness is not about being strong and
consistent in every work you do its about the
world seeing you as a real person. The real
firmness is only possible with nature of your
mighty personality.
That is the moment even if your breath stops on
this earth,you will be still alive in the history and
future. Live the moment.
Have ability and stability towards your target.
Be a true Human.
Being Empathatic and Honest are the two major
mirrors of life.

WHEN YOU WANT YOUR
CAREER TO BE
PERFECT THEN ACCEPT
THE FAILURES THAT
MADE YOU
IMPERFECT!
ONCE YOU
FAIL, STAND UP
AND TRY AGAIN UNTIL
YOU REACH IT BUT NEVER

GIVE UP!
MAKE YOUR
LIFE A SUCCESS JOURNEY
TO BE THE ENDLESS
DESTINY.
Consistency over Perfection. The hardest climb in your life is working on for yourself. All we need is a Hard work with a Bundle of Confidence,Struggle, Consistency and Will Power.
Aim High,Dream High and move forward to face the toughest challenges. Don't be afraid to fail,be afraid not to give up. Don't get upset,Failures are the stepping stones of Success. Make it like a best of both worlds.

Tear

Let every Scar on your chest heal you. You are
the best my sunshine.
A stultifying experience
carry a vary of emotional and physical violence.
You always laugh harder like you are about to
cry
Most days your mind don't ask why
A wave of light is an assurance
from thought of heart disturbance is a sign of
essence
You made your heart torn & mourn
 but your pulse make you own
Just listen,
Everything is a lesson.
Walk away from it with a perseverance
That is a positivity of elegance.
Everything is a blessing in disguise.

Don't Cry, Be You and have a Hope

Cry, cry and cry
Until your heart gets tired of your emotions.
Break down and let your pain pull you down
Until you heart knows your struggle.

In the beginning she got wounded,
looking at herself she cried.
Tears rolling down her cheeks
her pain made her worse gradually.
Pulse pounding in head & heart,
her eyes began to search for the hope.
Though her energy is sapped
She was strained making an effort,
but she strived against her strength.
Then later,whenever heart gotta prompt her, she
shook her legs vigorously at the time she heard a
loud inner voice."
And that's where the moment
"She ran for herself to get better. Yes, her
stamina heals her."

Never loose Hope!

MOOD

Though its heavy we let it go with Loneliness.
Breaking our own hearts by ourselves being so
careless.
The choice of weakness chose to be a part in
habit of happiness.
Trying out to be necessarily strong to save
myself.
The scary mind was so hard as hammer stabbing
my head.
The emotions,the feelings started bleeding.

In the mood of completely lost and broken,
you are tired of being strong
you are feeling worst and there is no one to talk
with and literally not even one to understand
you.

It hurts,it hurts the most where it lasts like you
wear your tear everyday with a smile. Loving
yourself
and crying at the same time.
Even yet you feel like a regret
at the time you want to forget
where you just kept hitting up your sweat
 when your eyes got wet

and everything that made you upset left with a disappointment.
In the end I own to be alone.
A tearful conversation between a Breathless heart and an Overthinking mind.
This is the hardest part someone could really feel.

Dear Heart

Believe yourself.

 She always desired to wish for her life to be
with the constant calmness and the ethical
promises.
I allowed my mind and heart to give voice for
my struggle.
Giving the self strength at the low self esteem
times.
Oh my Heart, Lets Talk!
You are Strong and you will be Strong.You have
that Strength.So, Stay Strong.
Let's Fight, & Fight from every burn of your
pain.
You came across a fallen tree
 you see a flying bee
You heard the branches whisper to you
 and the wind blew
In the sky,the birds flew
In the green fields
 The peace of leaves
grew so harder
Roots run deep
As the air began to weep.
 Entangled soul of this earth,
Am sure you will win this Battle.
Don't be afraid of your storms.

Your tear is really precious.
You and the chaos you carry. A hurricane on two legs.
So don't cry for the hurdles that you are facing.
Nothing hits the ground without an echo.
You are a Thunder.
Let's cross it with the Brave Heart.
To love & hope
To dream and believe in miracles
To rise from ashes and to grow again.
Your will power is your inner Strength.
Let's Go.
You are a Warrior.

What is my Life?

In the oceans of blue
At the deepest parts of my heart
My life is like a storm
In the waves of beautiful shore
My breathe is like a warmth
In the horizons of coast
Underneath the breezes
 The wide of feels
  The tide of seas
The pride of extremes
At the glory of my thoughts
In the calmness of my smiles
And my soul at the miles
Just Sparkle

Deep

When the time comes to harvest all my pain
I chose to pick up the petals
And lay them out to dry.

Am broken like a shattered glass
the heartache ignite a fire inside.

I bleed from the veins of struggle
Trauma crushing the chest.

The hell and heaven at once.
The circumstance of ironic all the time.

Like a breath of fresh air
and then took the breath away.

In deep
I wish I could explain myself how sensible I am.
I just need a soul
to understand what my heart is feeling
Just tearing up the paper of Tear that drained me
off.

I Hope,
When things don't work out.
Relax.Breathe in.
Just keep calm and enclose everything.
Let it go with the flow.
Good things do take time.

Why do I write?

I do write I do write and I will write where there
is so much to write
And yes,there is so much to Let out the things.
And yes, there are some Pocket of Mistakes and
Bunch of Regrets.
 and hell yeah, this is an Ocean of Secret in me
fighting with Hundreds of unanswered
questions.
But I always do respect and value myself
because am
Thankful for everything that has happened been
a
Blessing till now.

The every emotion from heart is drifted in ink on
the paper. The literature inside me inspired me to
utter the phrases.

It's okay.

In the process of consoling my heart everytime, I end up getting drained excessively.

Let every situation be what it is instead of having an imagination about it.
Just move on and let Destiny decide and show you the right path.

Sometimes It's okay to be Fragile
Get hurt & cry and drain in pain.
But don't forget to choose yourself in hard times too.
Never loose yourself. You are not lost you have to be found by yourself. Deal yourself because you are Strong.
You are this and you are the Best.
Don't run away.
Take the opportunity and Let the dimensions in you pass away.
Just Blossom.

Hey You.

Buddy,
Please Be Happy.
Don't ruin your future with your past in the
present.
There is so much to See, so much to go through.
You will definitely Shine like a Star
So, wait for the Brighter days.

An Evergreen Nature.
The Blue Sky and the Sunrise.
One day the sun was shining bright
A little more Daisy.
A girl in the park blinking her eyes with a spark
She was charming like a blossomed flower.
The rain began to sprinkle onto the ground
A Rainbow of colors way up high,
Birds chirping and a couple of butterflies
fluttered around the garden
Trees,plants,flowers around
The leaves fallen on the ground.
A new wind blows.
Then clouds came along and it was dark as night
and day goes.
Her Aura is made up of Roses but she is more
like a Thunderstorm.

She screams inside but for once she wants to be
heard.
She stayed up through the night because that is
when moon and her have conversations. The
place where she finds her peace.
All the words she hides behind her neck,there
are stories in her curves.
She was water before she became a fire from her
own ashes.
Quenching the thirst she puts her heartache first.
She turned from sea to desert.
She is both beautiful and terrible, and she
deserve someone who treats her like the moon
and can love the dark side of her soul too.
The stars glowing up like a hope for her looking
at her scars of chaos.
The tiny white crystals made her smile.
When she close her eyes she feels fulfilled.

Be Strong

I am Struggling but not being able to tell
anyone.
Finding it difficult to ask for help but feeling
overly responsible for others to give guidance
and fixing them.

Supressing the needs,thoughts and feelings.
Feeling lonely because no one really knows
what actually I am feeling.

Being very hard on myself and being
overwhelmed with the tasks.

And sometimes its okay and its totally fine when
you try to convince yourself and cry out loud
and still console your Heart for building up the
Self
Strength and yeah that's within you.

Be Thankful for everything that happened even
the most and most hidden battles too that you
fought for.
Yes, you are a Warrior. Be Strong.

The wrong decisions in your life
are the best lessons of your life.

Feel blessed for the great experiences you had.
Learn from your mistakes,
have a change in you
and make yourself a better version.

The little girl

Underneath the Tides running with a wave of
Million thoughts a weepy heartbeat says it all.
She took a nap and closed her eyes for a while.

The little girl had a dream last night.
She felt the touch of a kind soul giving her the
shoulder to cry on and lap to lie on.
Soothing her hair gently,holding her hands more
like an assurance,
she secured an immense love like a bliss.
She acquired a lot of comfort
something good was bound to happen she could
feel it in her bones.
All you need is a Warm Hug to Heal you. One
can really feel the bond of an attachment.
Holding each other's hands with full of
togetherness being there for one another.

After she dreamt,she woke up from lap of her
mother.
She realized that she could feel all the warmness
from her. She broke her eyes into tears.

Her parents raised her with pure values and
ethics. She has grown up like a queen nurtured
like a princess.
She could sense the comfort. She was safe and
snug in her arms.
She loves the way her father kisses her on the
forehead.
She could feel so complete from all their
love,care and affection genuinely. Its a lifetime
promise for her.
She was relieved and made her environment so
pleasant all over.
She started to heal herself from the aura of
positivity she has around.
Then,she smiled again.

A Heal from Depression and Anxiety

Just needed a Heart Talk with my Human Diary.
I wish I could find a twin soul like me.
So that I would give Immense Love for myself.
Being like a depressed soul when your health is
totally deteriorated!

- **What is Anxiety?**

Anxiety grips me in its hold
Its tendrils grow, ever bold
Every sound is amplified
Pain inside my head resides

My mind screams, my heart whispers low
My pulse beats fast, a constant flow
I self-deceive and try to hide and pretend
But the agony won't come to an end

I punch the wall, my hand in pain
Count my flaws, stare at the mirror again
Tears stream down, I feel so weak
Stress seeps through, it won't let me speak
Strangely and deliberately.
Chills run down my quivering spine

My mind races, like a frantic feline
A tremor shakes me to the core
A parched throat, can't take it anymore

Anxiety grips me, ever so tight
I struggle to get through each day and night
But I know I'll overcome this strife
And find the strength to live my life.

'It's feeling everything at once than feeling
paralysing numb.'

*The time when you get panic with your anxiety.
Usually it occurs unexpectedly and may have
specific triggers too. You have jerks in your
body while your trauma runs in your brain.
As much as its in your head its in your stomach
too.
You sweat outside but you die inside.
You loose your mind with breathlessness.
Everything looks so terrible that's about to
happen. You feel and sense about it. You notice
being disrupted and insomniac.
Builds severe nervousness and intensity. You
can't focus on one thing extremely.
Running and trying to get out.
Your heart throb begin to raise up.
You feel so like its going to stop.

Insecurities strains you with aggression in the whole body that pinches you on the nerves.

- **Here are some tips and ways to overcome the Panic and Anxiety Attacks**

You feel all the symptoms at once just relax.
Get out of your head and breathe.
Wrap your arms tightly around the person who is with you. It allows you to calm your mind.
They may resist and but at some point of time they will relax.
Try to sooth them and tell them it's gonna be okay.

Just remember your Strengths.
 Thoughts are just thoughts and you don't need to give meaning to them
Understand why you're feeling anxious, don't just accept your anxiety.
You can change the way you think.
Recognize about what you are and practice mindfulness.

•Do meditation for relaxation and concentration.
•Try to exercise,any other physical activity.
•Read a book, spend time focusing at your hobbies.

•Just write something,keep a journal to organize
your thoughts and feelings. Try to express
yourself.
Know about yourself completely.
•Get explored,go outside on a trips,socialize
with your friends and family.
See the nature and take a breath tell yourself that
everything is gonna be alright and you deserve
to be happy.
*It helps you to clear and improve the mind.
All of these can decrease your worry. It will
deviate you from the negative thoughts and
Overthinking.
Everything is in your hands fight with it.

Just Smile and try making time for yourself.
Find in depth what you are upto.
Learn to Enjoy being alone.
In a Loop for today we Realize
Later we regret.

State of being Bewildered is a Putative reason
for
A phase of Inexplicability And a cause of
Susceptibility!

"YOUR SELF THERAPY CAN HEAL YOU"

A wave of finding Peace.

Yes,am trying to enjoy.
Am trying to find happiness in little things like
how I use to do before.
Am laughing out so loud.
Just trying to breath the present with positivity.
Don't know what happens next,
But I feel atleast I should be happy for today.
Even am Sad Inside, I will try to be Happy
Outside and keep my people Happy around me.

Just take control of your thoughts.
Even that needs a lot of strength.
Being physically and mentally strong is the
difficult one but it needs lot of efforts and
practice.

In the beginning it can make you so hard but
eventually whenever it gets habituated to your
routine life you will start accepting the things.
Fix a fact of everything is temporary and
nothing is permanent.
Say it to yourself that 'this incident is only for
today and tomorrow its over because its past.'
So,just think about the next goals you want to
do. Don't think about what had happened behind

your back,live in what is happening and plan about what has to happen. That is present and future.

This is not me.

An anguished Story.

Being always lost in your own thoughts,

Eventually nobody cares and Nobody really
knows what someone going through in their life.
One can be in a very vulnerable state feeling so
desperated.
The very hard times make you feel so worse.
Every so often you feel like you're missing
yourself so much!
You miss the old version of you, especially the
way you are!
Crying over and over again,
Deeper than deeper,
You heart knows that you are Strong but you
always need someone to talk to you and take
care of you.
You always need someone to love you
unconditionally.
You always need someone to hold your hands,
give you a shoulder and pamper you all the time.
You always need that tight hug and forehead kiss
whenever you feel low.
All you need is Love to Heal you.

You really need a deep conversations while
sitting on the roof tops and looking at the stars.
Happiness had been a mess.
Being like a faded smile,
You really want to smile again with a whole
heart.

Just Fly

When i fell down, I didn't drown. i chose to Fly,
I chose to swim for my life, To the new
beginnings where I fell in Love with a Pure
Soul.
Yes, that's with Myself.
I Wish I deserve this, may be in the Parallel
World I am Happy with what I have Hope for.

Eliminate your Regrets, Find a way for
forgiveness,
Be Transparent.
Spread Your Wings, Fly high and Make your
Life Colourful.

The Pain

Am crying,am crying,am crying until I get tired.
Since so many days am fed up of crying
but my tears couldn't stop rolling down my
cheeks. I feel pity for myself.
I am Fighting, I am fighting and fighting until
the person inside me gives up. I am fighting.
And Yes, I should heal I must heal and I will
heal until my wound turns into my Strength.

I am terrified by this dark thing that sleeps in me
and stays in my soul.
Life is not always in our favor it mostly shows
the cruel shade of it to make us stronger than
before.

The monsters were never outside. They were
inside my head thriving on chaos. The big
tragedy spirit.
I am type of flower that still grows after a forest
fire.

A Fiduciary

This is paining. The patience is tearing.
In a low state The wait is falling down.
Though my Heart is wounded,
somewhere it is still waiting for the Hope.
Draining out with the struggles inside I feel like
giving up many times but still I find myself in
the drains where no one could ever heal my pain
nor I could imagine a happy life.
Believing that Time Heals Everything.
A Dreamgoal is nothing without a Trust.
Yes, I am Strong.

Am the Strength

A Pain from my Every Vein
Again I Gain
Falling apart Insane
I always remain Drain
I overcame at the time of Exclaim
Yes, over a period now I Proclaim,
I Am Vigorously an Indestructible Soul!

Happiness

'START GROWING'

Every person is Strong enough to let it go, we
must pick up the pieces and start over.
I started growing up with vulnerability.
A pain can not only heal you,it will make you
stronger than ever.
Wounds are the best lessons. It may harm you
now but later it will heal you.
Distress is a Bless.
One can understand if they are an injured
person.
Make your every chapter a challenge.
All you need is a peace of mind. No amount of
guilt can change the past
and no amount of anxiety can change the future.
Its about creating yourself.
I learnt that a bird in hand is worth two in the
bush.

Happiness is my only choice.
But being Happy or Sad were part of my
journey.
Finally, The End.
I really wanna look back once &
Thank. Am grateful for what I am today.

I overcame the hardships.
I Fought for what I really wanted to be.
Gone through with shades of emotional phases..
Where I drained with my internal battles that
gave me the strength externally
Where my every tear had bursted out all the
hurdles of pain I had.
But I never gave up.
Thank you for making me more stronger than
enough from volcano of my emotions.
 I always believe in "When you can't control
what's happening,challenge yourself to control
the way you are responding to what's happening.
That's where the power is."

YES,I WON MYSELF.

THE END.

{Its over for now.
A lot more with a full stop.}
Ending this volume with a bright smile.
To be continued..

-BHASRUTHA REDDY